DEAR HUMANS

A Letter from the Animals

Written by Nisha Coleman

Illustrated by Shanthony Exum

LINDA LEITH PUBLISHING

Gorilla is noticing changes all around.

Something isn't right. The days are hotter. It's raining more than usual.

The forest is shrinking. Are animals in other parts of the world experiencing changes too?

There is only one way to find out.

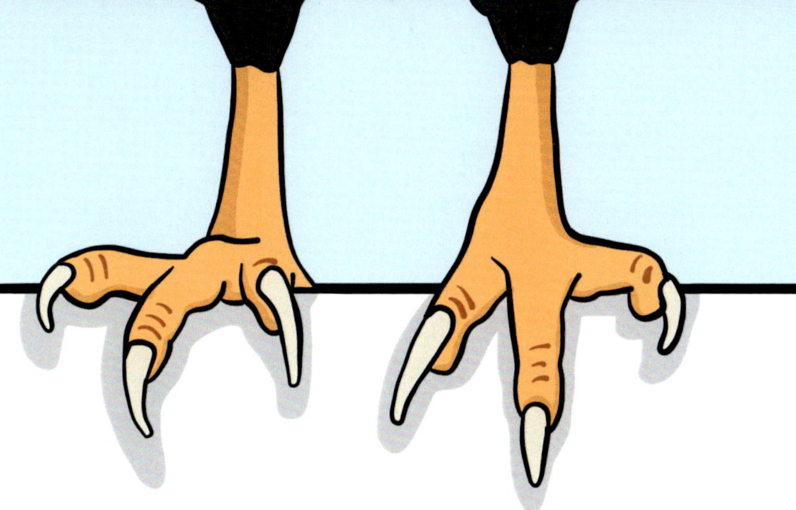

Urgent:
Your presence is needed!

You are invited to a Global Animal Summit to discuss the environmental changes in our homes and what we can do about them.

Where: Gorilla's mountain home

When: Summer solstice

The journey is long, but I believe our planet is in peril.

Sincerely,
Gorilla

They come. From water, skies, and forests.
Over mountains, through meadows, and past volcanoes.
Animals arrive from every part of the world.

"It is an honour to welcome you all to my misty mountains," says Gorilla.
"My home is lush, with delicious leaves and succulent bamboo.
But humans are cutting down trees for farms and digging up earth for mines.
The forest is disappearing, and the sun is burning hotter than ever."

“Please, tell me what is happening where you live.”

Polar Bear is first to speak.

"I come from a frozen land. Instead of trees, we have snow and rolling tundra.
My family and I hunt for food on the sea ice.
Sometimes colourful lights dance in the night sky.
It is a peaceful life in my snowy wonderland."

"But the sea ice is melting,
which means we have to swim farther and farther to find food.
More and more, we come home tired and hungry."

Gazelle's tail flicks.

"I come from the savanna.
It's a wonderful place with wide open grassy land, lots of small trees,
and watering holes where all kinds of animals drink together.
It is an exciting place to live
because everyone is always travelling."

“But the temperature is rising fast.
The trees that once sheltered us from the piercing sun
and blowing sand have disappeared.
The grass is burning and the watering holes are drying up.
Every year, more sand takes over. My savanna is turning into a desert.
Eventually, I will have nowhere to go.”

Tortoise's head slowly lifts.

"I come from the sea. I will speak for water.
The sparkling lakes, the flowing rivers, the vast oceans.
Water connects all living creatures and is always in motion.
Water is a source of life for everybody, including humans."

“But humans use massive fishing nets to scrape the bottom of the seas.
They take too many fish and crack the precious coral.
Farms and factories leak poison into our water.
Plastic is piling up in lakes and oceans.
Sometimes we get tangled in it, or eat it by mistake.”

Toucan's wings stretch out wide.

"I come from the tropical rainforest. It has the tallest trees you can imagine and vines that grow everywhere. Half of the Earth's plant and animal species can be found in my home. It is bursting with life and colour."

"But something terrible is happening.
Humans are cutting and burning the forest to plant crops and raise cattle.
Without the trees, the land turns hard and dry.
Then they cut more trees! We're scared of losing our only home."

“So humans are behind all this!”
cries Polar Bear. “They are ruining everything!”

Gazelle agrees.
“Humans are the problem and must be stopped right away!”

“I heard they have rocket ships,”
says Toucan. “Let’s send them to another planet!”

“Yes,” says Tortoise.
“They don’t deserve to be here!”

“Wait!” cries a small voice. “I haven’t spoken yet.”

Tabby Cat leaps onto a high branch.

"I come from the city. I live with a human family that feeds me and takes care of me. I have a good life. I play in the garden and explore the alleys with my friends. Sometimes we climb trees in the park or play hide-and-seek. The city is full of buzzing energy. It's an exciting place to live."

"But the little boy in my family isn't well.
His lungs are sick from poison in the air.
Every morning he needs medicine to help him breathe.
On hot summer days, he's not allowed to go outside
because the air is thick and yucky."

“I see,” says Gorilla. “Humans are suffering too.”

“Why don’t they do something?” asks Polar Bear.

“They must not be very smart!” says Gazelle.

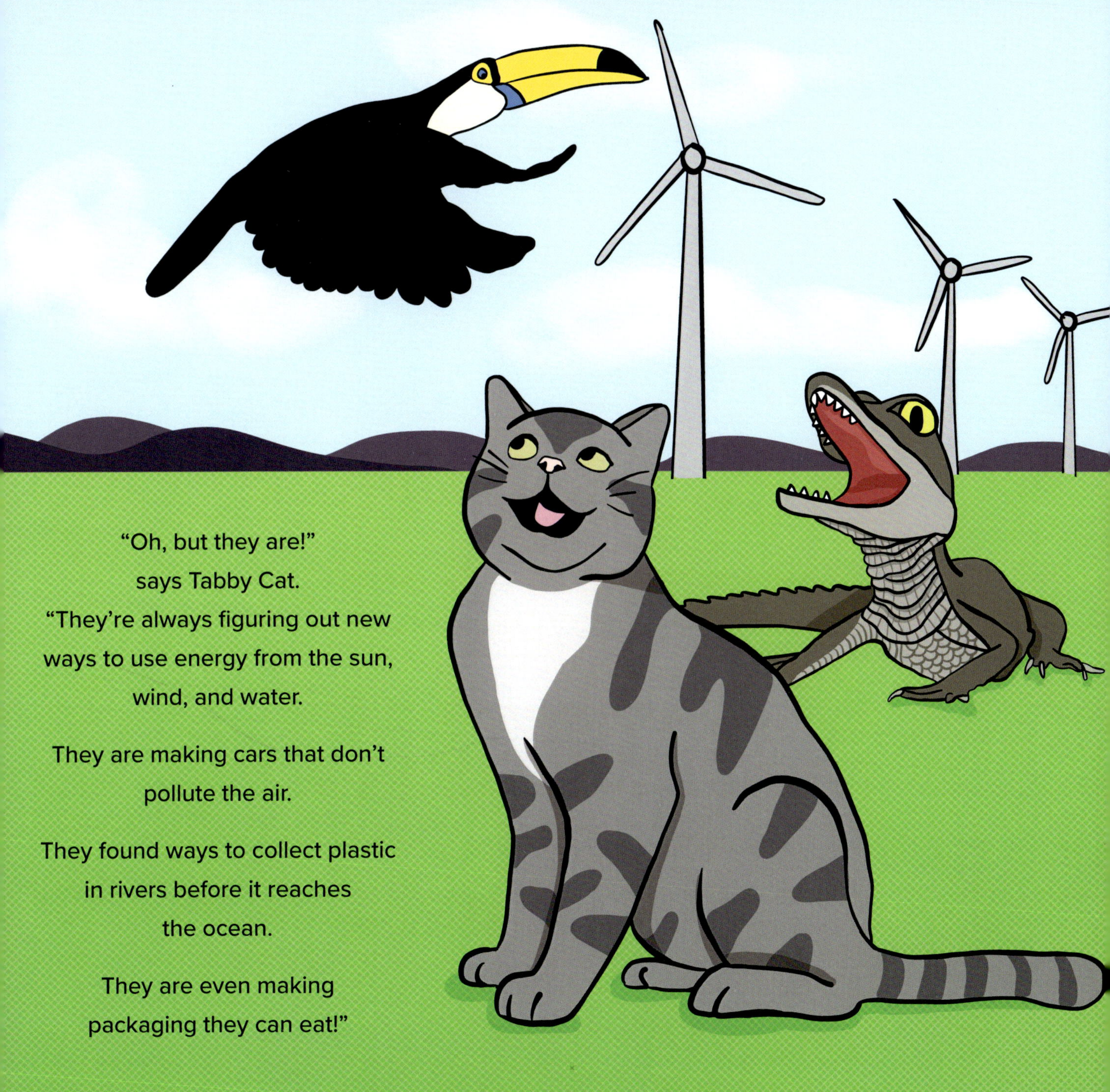

"Oh, but they are!" says Tabby Cat. "They're always figuring out new ways to use energy from the sun, wind, and water.

They are making cars that don't pollute the air.

They found ways to collect plastic in rivers before it reaches the ocean.

They are even making packaging they can eat!"

"Then why are they still polluting so much? Don't they care?"

"Some of them do," says Toucan. "There are humans who live with us in the rainforest in perfect harmony with nature. They are careful with what they take and what they leave behind."

"Now that you mention it," says Polar Bear, "I've seen humans who respect the fish they catch and never take more than they need."

“From what you are saying,” says Gorilla,
“humans have an ancient wisdom that still thrives,
as well as modern and creative ways to solve problems.
Why aren’t they working together to fix this?”

"They are distracted by money," says Tabby Cat. "They talk about it all the time. They think that having money and buying new things will make them happy."

Gazelle snorts. "How could money make anyone happy? I have never had money, but I am very happy. Or at least I was until my savanna started to dry up."

"Maybe they forgot what makes creatures on Earth happy," suggests Polar Bear.

“In that case,” says Toucan, “we must remind them.”

“Good idea,” says Gorilla. “Something that makes me happy is the cool mountain mist rising in the morning. It makes me feel calm and peaceful.”

"For me," says Polar Bear, "tumbling in freshly fallen snow with my family makes me happy."

"I love the bright colours of the coral reef and the dazzling fish that live there," says Tortoise.

"I love sitting in the garden watching butterflies dance and the strawberries turn red," says Tabby Cat. "Cuddling with my human family at night makes me purr with joy."

“Meeting new friends at the watering hole makes me happy,” says Gazelle. “I love hearing their stories from distant lands.”

"Listening to the music of the forest
is my favourite thing to do,"
says Toucan.
"The rain hitting the leaves,
the humming insects,
the monkeys laughing together."

"The more humans spend time in nature,
the more they will love and understand it,"
says Tortoise. "Then they will stop filling it with plastic."

“They will plant more trees than they take.”

“They will grow their own food and meet farmers to get food that grows nearby.”

"They will stop eating so many animals and fish."

"They will stop using chemicals that ruin the water and cars that poison the air."

“Instead of always buying things new,
they will trade with each other,
and learn to repair and even make things themselves.
The way they used to.”

“If they spend more time outside,
they will see more comets and stars and sunsets and rainbows.”

“Instead of just hearing the wind, they will listen to it.
They will learn nature’s language.”

"Then they will be truly happy."

Gorilla rises. “Let’s write to the humans. We must warn them. Before it’s too late.”

“Wait!” shouts Gazelle. “How can we trust them?”

“We have no choice,” says Gorilla.
“They have to fix their mess and find new ways to live. We are all at risk—even them.”

"And if they don't listen?"

"Then,"

says Toucan,

"we'll go to Plan B."

URGENT: Immediate action required

Dear Humans,

You have forgotten how to belong here.

You have forgotten all the things the Earth gives you for free.

Can you work together to help us make the Earth happy again?

When the Earth is happy, we can all be happy together.

Sincerely,
The Animals

P.S. If you do not do as we ask, we will have no choice but to send you to another planet. And it will not be even half as wonderful as Earth.

Nisha Coleman - Author

Nisha Coleman grew up in a forest in Muskoka, Ontario, and now lives in Montreal, Quebec. Things that make her happy are seeing rainbows, going for walks in the forest, and watching the leaves change colour in the fall. She loves animals and is passionate about living lightly and making the Earth happy.

Shanthony Exum - Illustrator

Shanthony grew up in Charlotte, North Carolina, and now lives in Montreal, Quebec. Things that make her happy are drawing, paper mache, and cooking fresh vegetables. She loves finding new uses for things instead of throwing them away. Most of all, she enjoys walking in the park with her friends.